FIND OUT ABOUT
Wood

This edition 2002

© Franklin Watts 1994

Franklin Watts
96 Leonard Street
LONDON EC2A 4XD

Franklin Watts Australia
45-51 Huntley Street
Alexandria
NSW 2015

ISBN: 0 7496 4781 7

Dewey Decimal Classification 333.75

A CIP catalogue record for this book
is available from the British Library

Editor: Annabel Martin
Design: Thumb Design

Photographs: © English Heritage 19; Eye
Ubiquitous © Hugh Rooney 25 (inset); Chris
Fairclough Colour Library 6, 7, 8, 10, 11, 12, 13, 14,
15, 16, 17, 20, 21, 23, 25, 27, 29 (both); Robert
Harding Picture Library 22, © Christopher
Nicholson 24, © Sarah King 28; The Hutchison
Library 30, © Edward Parker 4, © Val Whelan 9,
© John Wright 31; National Trust Photographic
Library 18, © J. Whitaker 26; ZEFA 5.

Printed in Hong Kong, China

FIND OUT ABOUT
Wood

Henry Pluckrose

W

FRANKLIN WATTS
LONDON•SYDNEY

Wood comes from trees.
Trees grow all over the world.
They grow in hot, damp
lands of Africa, Asia
and South America.

They also grow in lands where winters are very cold.

In some countries
forests are specially planted.
Saplings, which are little trees,
are planted in long rows.

When they are fully grown, the trees are cut down. The branches are trimmed from the trees.

At the saw mill,
the trunks are cut into planks ...

and dried.
Dried wood is called timber.

Many different tools
are used for cutting
and shaping wood.
Saws cut it,
planes smooth it,
chisels cut into it
and decorate it,
lathes turn and shape it,
drills make holes in it.

Most of the tools
we use to shape timber
are made of metal.
Can you think why?

Pieces of wood can be fixed together with nails, screws or glue.

Another way of fixing
pieces of wood together
is to make a joint.
The shapes cut into each
piece of wood
fit neatly into each other.

Woodwork must be protected from water, rain and sun. Wooden things are painted to prevent them from rotting.

Furniture is waxed and polished to protect the wooden surface from spills of food and drink.

Wood is a very useful material. It can be used in many ways — to build real houses ...

and to make toy ones!

Most wood is tough
and long lasting.
This table is over 500 years old...

and this chair was made
long before your grandmother
was born.

Many other things in our homes
are made from wood –
the handles of brushes, brooms,
kitchen knives, cooking spoons,
salad and fruit bowls,
cutting boards.

Why do we use a wooden mat
to protect a polished table
from a hot dish?
The metal spoon lets heat
pass through it easily.
Metal is a good conductor of heat.
The wooden handle
stays cool because
wood is a poor conductor of heat.

Wood floats.
Long before people made
boats of metal,
there were boats
made from wood.

Wood is a tough material.
It is used to build quays
where ships tie up
to unload their cargo.

Some kinds of wheels are still made from wood. The rim of the wheel is given a metal shoe to prevent the wood from wearing away.

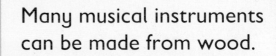

Many musical instruments can be made from wood.

Wood is soft enough
to carve.
Some old houses
are decorated with
wood carvings.
This carving was made
over 300 years ago.

Wood is also used to make decorations for people. Would you like to wear these beads?

It is surprising how many ways
we use wood.
In this factory, wood is
crushed into tiny pieces
and mixed with water
and chemicals.
The mixture is dried
in thin, smooth sheets,
called paper.
Paper is made from wood.

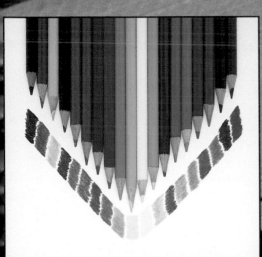

We even need wood to make pencils!

Trees which give us wood
take many years to grow.
In some parts of the world,
large areas of forests
are being cut down.
The wood is sold
and the land left empty.

When this happens,
the soil is often washed away
and nothing can grow.
We must learn to care
for the world of nature.
Can you imagine
the countryside with no trees?

About this book

This book is designed for use in the home, kindergarten and infant school.

Parents can share the book with young children. Its aim is to bring into focus some of the elements of life and living which are all too often taken for granted. To develop fully, all young children need to have their understanding of the world deepened and the language they use to express their ideas extended. This book, and others in the series, takes the everyday things of the child's world and explores them, harnessing curiosity and wonder in a purposeful way.

For those working with young children each book is designed to be used both as a picture book, which explores ideas and concepts, and as a starting point to talk and exploration. The pictures have been selected because they are of interest in themselves and also because they include elements which will promote enquiry. Talk can lead to displays of items and pictures collected by children and teacher. Pictures and collages can be made by the children themselves.

Everything in our environment is of interest to the growing child. The purpose of these books is to extend and develop that interest.

Henry Pluckrose